WORDS OF THANKSGIVING:

Prayers, Poems and Meditations
for the Month of November

© 2012 by Xist Publishing
Illustrations are licensed from Fotolia
ISBN-13: 978-1-62395-441-3

All rights reserved
No portion of this book may be reproduced without express permission of the publisher
All images licensed from Fotolia
First Edition

Published in the United States by Xist Publishing
www.xistpublishing.com
PO Box 61593 Irvine, CA 92602

Words of Thanksgiving

Prayers, Poems and Meditations for the Month of November

edited by Nancy Streza

Contents

Thanksgiving	6
We Gather Together	7
For The Beauty Of The Earth	8
Come, Ye Thankful People, Come	10
Psalm 95	12
Count Your Blessings	13
We Give You Thanks	14
Thanksgiving Address	15
A Thanksgiving	16
1 Chronicles 29: 10-13	19
All Good Gifts	20
Accept, O Lord	22
Heap High	24
A Grateful Heart	25
Thanksgiving Day	26
A Thankful Strain	27
Now Thank We All Our God	28
Full Circle	30
Glory to God for	31
All Things	31
Morning Thanksgiving	32
Count Your Blessings	33
Father, We Thank Thee	34
Thanksgiving	36
Over the River and Through the Woods	38

Thanksgiving

Ralph Waldo Emerson

For each new morning with its light,
For rest and shelter of the night,
For health and food,
For love and friends,
For everything Thy goodness sends.
For flowers that bloom about our feet;
For tender grass, so fresh, so sweet;
For song of bird, and hum of bee;
For all things fair we hear or see,
Father in heaven, we thank Thee!

We Gather Together

Adrianus Valerius
Translation by Theodore Baker

We gather together to ask the Lord's blessing;
He chastens and hastens his will to make known;
The wicked oppressing now cease from distressing,
Sing praises to his name: He forgets not his own.

Beside us to guide us, our God with us joining,
Ordaining, maintaining his kingdom divine;
So from the beginning the fight we were winning;
Thou, Lord, wast at our side, All glory be thine!

We all do extol thee, thou leader triumphant,
And pray that thou still our defender wilt be.
Let thy congregation escape tribulation;
Thy name be ever praised! O Lord, make us free!

For The Beauty Of The Earth

Folliot.S Pierpoint

For the beauty of the earth
For the glory of the skies,
For the love which from our birth
Over and around us lies.

Lord of all, to Thee we raise,
This our hymn of grateful praise.

For the beauty of each hour,
Of the day and of the night,
Hill and vale, and tree and flower,
Sun and moon, and stars of light.

Lord of all, to Thee we raise,
This our hymn of grateful praise.

For the joy of ear and eye,
For the heart and mind's delight,
For the mystic harmony
Linking sense to sound and sight.

Lord of all, to Thee we raise,
This our hymn of grateful praise.

For the joy of human love,
Brother, sister, parent, child,
Friends on earth and friends above,
For all gentle thoughts and mild.

Lord of all, to Thee we raise,
This our hymn of grateful praise.

For each perfect gift of Thine,
To our race so freely given,
Graces human and divine,
Flowers of earth and buds of Heaven.

Lord of all, to Thee we raise,
This our hymn of grateful praise.

Come, Ye Thankful People, Come

Henry Alford

Come, ye thankful people, come,
Raise the song of harvest home!
All is safely gathered in,
Ere the winter storms begin;
God, our Maker, doth provide
For our wants to be supplied;
Come to God's own temple, come;
Raise the song of harvest home!

We ourselves are God's own field,
Fruit unto his praise to yield;
Wheat and tares together sown
Unto joy or sorrow grown;
First the blade and then the ear,
Then the full corn shall appear;
Grant, O harvest Lord, that we
Wholesome grain and pure may be.

For the Lord our God shall come,
And shall take the harvest home;
From His field shall in that day
All offenses purge away,
Giving angels charge at last
In the fire the tares to cast;
But the fruitful ears to store
In the garner evermore.

Then, thou Church triumphant come,
Raise the song of harvest home!
All be safely gathered in,
Free from sorrow, free from sin,
There, forever purified,
In God's garner to abide;
Come, ten thousand angels, come,
Raise the glorious harvest home!

Psalm 95

O come, let us sing unto the LORD:
let us make a joyful noise to the rock of our salvation.
Let us come before his presence with thanksgiving, and make a joyful noise unto him with psalms.
For the LORD is a great God, and a great King above all gods. In his hand are the deep places of the earth:
the strength of the hills is his also. The sea is his, and he made it: and his hands formed the dry land.
O come, let us worship and bow down: let us kneel before the LORD our maker.

Count Your Blessings

Author Unknown

Count your blessings instead of your crosses;
Count your gains instead of your losses.
Count your joys instead of your woes;
Count your friends instead of your foes.
Count your smiles instead of your tears;
Count your courage instead of your fears.
Count your full years instead of your lean;
Count your kind deeds instead of your mean.
Count your health instead of your wealth;
Count on God instead of yourself.

We Give You Thanks

Book of Common Prayer

Almighty and gracious Father,
we give you thanks
for the fruits of the earth in their season
and for the labors of those who harvest them.
Make us, we pray,
faithful stewards of your great bounty,
for the provision of our necessities
and the relief of all who are in need,
to the glory of your Name;
through Jesus Christ our Lord,
who lives and reigns with
you and the Holy Spirit,
one God, now and for ever. Amen.

Thanksgiving Address

Abraham Lincoln

No human counsel hath devised nor hath any mortal hand worked out these great things. They are the gracious gifts of the Most High God, who, while dealing with us in anger for our sins, hath nevertheless remembered mercy. It has seemed to me fit and proper that they should be solemnly, reverently and gratefully acknowledged as with one heart and one voice by the whole American People. I do therefore invite my fellow citizens in every part of the United States, and also those who are at sea and those who are sojourning in foreign lands, to set apart and observe the last Thursday of November next, as a day of Thanksgiving and Praise to our beneficent Father who dwelleth in the Heavens.

A Thanksgiving

George MacDonald

I Thank Thee, boundless Giver,
That the thoughts Thou givest flow
In sounds that like a river
All through the darkness go.
And though few should swell the pleasure,
By sharing this my wine,
My heart will clasp its treasure,
This secret gift of Thine.

My heart the joy inherits,
And will oft be sung to rest;
And some wandering hoping spirits
May listen and be blest.
For the sound may break the hours
In a dark and gloomy mood,
As the wind breaks up the bowers
Of the brooding sunless wood.

For every sound of gladness
　　Is a prophet-wind that tells
Of a summer without sadness,
　　And a love without farewells;
And a heart that hath no ailing,
　　And an eye that is not dim,
And a faith that without failing
　　Shall be complete in Him.

And when my heart is mourning,
　　The songs it lately gave,
Back to their fount returning,
　　Make sweet the bitter wave;
And forth a new stream floweth,
　　In sunshine winding fair;
And through the dark wood goeth
　　Glad laughter on the air.

For the heart of man that waketh,
　　Yet hath not ceased to dream,
Is the only fount that maketh
　　The sweet and bitter stream.
But the sweet will still be flowing
　　When the bitter stream is dry,
And glad music only going
　　On the breezes of the sky.

I thank Thee, boundless Giver,
That the thoughts Thou givest flow
In sounds that like a river
All through the darkness go.
And though few should swell the pleasure
By sharing this my wine,
My heart will clasp its treasure,
This secret gift of Thine.

1 Chronicles 29: 10-13

Blessed be thou, LORD God of Israel our father, for ever and ever. Thine, O LORD is the greatness, and the power, and the glory, and the victory, and the majesty: for all that is in the heaven and in the earth is thine; thine is the kingdom, O LORD, and thou art exalted as head above all. Both riches and honour come of thee, and thou reignest over all; and in thine hand is power and might; and in thine hand it is to make great, and to give strength unto all. Now therefore, our God, we thank thee, and praise thy glorious name.

All Good Gifts

Matthias Claudius
Translated by Jane Mongomery Cambell

We plough the fields and scatter
The good seed on the land,
But it is fed and watered
By God's almighty hand:
He sends the snow in winter,
The warmth to swell the grain,
The breezes and the sunshine,
And soft, refreshing rain.

He only is the Maker
Of all things near and far;
He paints the wayside flower,
He lights the evening star;
The winds and waves obey him,
By him the birds are fed;
Much more to us, his children,
He gives our daily bread.

We thank thee then, O Father,
For all things bright and good,
The seed time and the harvest,
Our life, our health, our food.
Accept the gifts we offer
For all thy love imparts,
And what thou most desirest,
Our humble, thankful hearts.

All good gifts around us
Are sent from heaven above;
Then thank the Lord,
O thank the Lord,
For all his love.

Accept, O Lord
Book of Common Prayer

Accept, O Lord,
our thanks and praise for all that you have
done for us.
We thank you for the splendor of
the whole creation,
for the beauty of this world,
for the wonder of life,
and for the mystery of love.
We thank you for the blessing of
family and friends,
and for the loving care
which surrounds us on every side.
We thank you for setting us at tasks
which demand our best efforts,
and for leading us to accomplishments
which satisfy and delight us.

We thank you also
for those disappointments and failures
that lead us to acknowledge

our dependence on you alone.
Above all, we thank you for your Son Jesus Christ;
for the truth of his Word
and the example of his life;
for his steadfast obedience,
by which he overcame temptation;
for his dying,
through which he overcame death;
and for his rising to life again,
in which we are raised to the life of your kingdom.
Grant us the gift of your Spirit,
that we may know him and make him known;
and through him, at all times and in all places,
may give thanks to you in all things. Amen.

Heap High

Alice Williams Brotherton

Heap high the board with plenteous cheer,
And gather to the feast,
And toast the sturdy Pilgrim band
Whose courage never ceased.

Give praise to that All-Gracious One
By whom their steps were led,
And thanks unto the harvest's Lord
Who sends our daily bread.

A Grateful Heart

George Herbert

Thou hast given so much to me,
Give one thing more, - a grateful heart;
Not thankful when it pleaseth me,
As if Thy blessings had spare days,
But such a heart whose pulse may be Thy praise.

Thanksgiving Day
Emily Dickinson

One day is there of the series
Termed Thanksgiving day,
Celebrated part at table,
Part in memory.
Neither patriarch nor pussy,
I dissect the play;
Seems it, to my hooded thinking,
Reflex holiday.
Had there been no sharp subtraction
From the early sum,
Not an acre or a caption
Where was once a room,
Not a mention, whose small pebble
Wrinkled any bay,--
Unto such, were such assembly,
'T were Thanksgiving day.

A Thankful Strain

Alexander Pope

Our rural ancestors, with little blest,
Patient of labour when the end was rest,
Indulged the day that housed their annual grain,
With feasts, and off'rings, and a thankful strain.

Now Thank We All Our God

Martin Rinkart

Now thank we all our God
With hearts and hands and voices
Who wondrous things has done
In whom His world rejoices
Who from our mother's arms
Has blessed us on our way
With countless gifts of love
And still is ours today

O may this bounteous God
Thro' all our life be near us
With ever joyful hearts
And blessed peace to cheer us
And keep us in His grace
And guide us when perplexed
And free us from all ills
In this world and the next

All praise and thanks to God
The Father now be given
The Son and Him who reigns
With them in highest heaven
The one eternal God
Whom earth and heav'n adore
For thus it was is now
And shall be evermore

Full Circle
Author Unknown

The year has turned its circle,
The seasons come and go.
The harvest all is gathered in
And chilly north winds blow.
Orchards have shared their treasures,
The fields, their yellow grain,
So open wide the doorway
Thanksgiving comes again!

Glory to God for All Things

Prince Boris Petrovich Turkestanov

Glory to Thee for calling me into being
Glory to Thee, showing me the beauty
of the universe
Glory to Thee, spreading out before me
heaven and earth
Like the pages in a book of eternal wisdom
Glory to Thee for Thine eternity in this
fleeting world
Glory to Thee for Thy mercies, seen and unseen
Glory to Thee through every sigh of my sorrow
Glory to Thee for every step of my life's journey
For every moment of glory
Glory to Thee, O God, from age to age

Morning Thanksgiving

St. Augustine of Hippo

O God, the God of spirits and of all flesh,
Who is beyond compare, and stands in
need of nothing,
Who has given the sun to have rule over the day,
and the moon and the stars to have rule
over the night
now also look down upon us with gracious eyes,
and receive our morning thanksgivings, and have
mercy upon us;
for we have not "spread out our hands to a
strange God."
for there is not among us any new God, but You,
the eternal God,
Who are without end
Who has given us our being through Christ
and given us our well-being through Him.
Graciously grant us, through Him, eternal life
with whom glory and honor and worship
be to You and to the Holy Spirit forever and ever.
Amen

Count Your Blessings

Author Unknown

Count your blessings
Name them one by one
Count your blessings
See what God has done
Count your blessings
Name them one by one
And it will surprise you
What the Lord has done

Father, We Thank Thee

Author Unknown
(Often attributed to Ralph Waldo Emerson)

For flowers that bloom about our feet,
Father, we thank Thee.

For tender grass so fresh, so sweet,
Father, we thank Thee.

For the song of bird and hum of bee,
For all things fair we hear or see,
Father in heaven, we thank Thee.

For blue of stream and blue of sky,
Father, we thank Thee.

For pleasant shade of branches high,
Father, we thank Thee.

For fragrant air and cooling breeze,
For beauty of the blooming trees,
Father in heaven, we thank Thee.

For this new morning with its light,
Father, we thank Thee.

For rest and shelter of the night,
Father, we thank Thee

For health and food, for love and friends,
For everything Thy goodness sends,
Father in heaven, we thank Thee.

Thanksgiving

Kate Seymour Maclean

The Autumn hills are golden at the top,
    And rounded as a poet's silver rhyme;
The mellow days are ruby ripe, that drop
    One after one into the lap of time.

Dead leaves are reddening in the woodland copse,
    And forest boughs a fading glory wear;
No breath of wind stirs in their hazy tops,
    Silence and peace are brooding everywhere.

The long day of the year is almost done,
    And nature in the sunset musing stands,
Gray-robed, and violet-hooded like a nun,
    Looking abroad o'er yellow harvest lands:

O'er tents of orchard boughs, and purple vines
    With scarlet flecked, flung like broad banners out

Along the field paths where slow-pacing lines
　　Of meek-eyed kine obey the herdboy's shout;

Where the tired ploughman his dun oxen turns,
　　Unyoked, afield, mid dewy grass to stray,
While over all the village church spire burns--
　　A shaft of flame in the last beams of day.

　　Empty and folded are her busy hands;
　　Her corn and wine and oil are safely stored,
　　As in the twilight of the year she stands,
　　　　And with her gladness seems to thank
　　　　　　the Lord.

　　Thus let us rest awhile from toil and care,
　　　In the sweet sabbath of this autumn calm,
And lift our hearts to heaven in grateful prayer,
　　And sing with nature our thanksgiving psalm

Over the River and Through the Woods

Lydia Maria Child

Over the river and through the wood
To Grandmother's house we go.
The horse knows the way
To carry the sleigh
Through white and drifted snow.

Over the river and through the wood
Oh, how the wind does blow!
It stings the toes
And bites the nose,
As over the ground we go.

Over the river and through the wood
To have a first-rate play.
Hear the bells ring,
Ting-a-ling-ling!
Hurrah for Thanksgiving Day!

Over the river and through the wood,
Trot fast, my dapple gray!
Spring over the ground
Like a hunting hound,
For this is Thanksgiving Day.

Over the river and through the wood,
And straight through the barnyard gate.
We seem to go
Extremely slow~
It is so hard to wait!

Over the river and through the wood~
Now Grandmother's cap I spy!
Hurrah for fun!
Is the pudding done?
Hurrah for the pumpkin pie!

www.ingramcontent.com/pod-product-compliance
Lightning Source LLC
LaVergne TN
LVHW021600070426
835507LV00014B/1885